ADVICE TO MY 18-YEAR-OLD SELF

AN ESSAY COLLECTION

Asymmetrical Press
Missoula, Montana

Published by Asymmetrical Press, Missoula, Montana.

You have arrived at your destination.

Library of Congress Cataloging-in-Publication Data
Advice to my 18-year-old self — 1st ed.
ISBN: 978-1-938793-32-5
eISBN: 978-1-938793-33-2
WC: 14,522
1. Self-help. 2. Essays. 3.Advice. 4. Inspiration. 5. Life lessons.

Cover design by Colin Wright
Formatted in beautiful Montana
Printed in the U.S.A.
Typeset in Garamond

Publisher info:
Website: www.asymmetrical.co
Email: howdy@asymmetrical.co
Twitter: @asympress

ASYM METR ICAL

This book is dedicated to everyone
who wishes they could go back
and give their younger selves
some much-needed advice.

For every regret I have, the
thing I could have done was
just to try it. Do something that
makes you uncomfortable, scared, nervous.
Just try it. All of it. Anytime.
I wish I knew this at 18.
— Chris

ACKNOWLEDGMENTS

A great big thanks to…

You are only young once, but you can be immature for a lifetime.

—John Grier

ADVICE
TO
MY
18
YEAR
OLD
SELF

CONTENTS

SOME PLATITUDES
ARE KIND OF PROFOUND

Joshua Fields Millburn
Age 32

You can't change the people around you, but you can change the people around you. Slow down—emotions are faster than thoughts. Laugh a little. Laugh a lot. Your smile is contagious—go infect someone. Discover your interests, values, and beliefs; pursue those things, not what you're *supposed* to pursue. You become what you desire. You are what you love. *Love* is not the same thing as *like*. A person doesn't necessarily like you just because he or she *Liked* you on Facebook. It is possible to dislike certain parts of a person and still love every piece of them. Passion is one-half love, one-half obsession. Passion has virtually nothing to do with excitement. Become a slave to your craft if you want to be a master. Obsession leads to isolation, isolation to obsession. Obsession is neither inherently good nor inherently bad. It is not ambition that sets a man apart; it is the distance he is prepared to go. Every path is a shortcut when you're stuck in neutral. Don't let your crastination turn pro. It takes just a little light to displace the darkness. You've won when your dreams have broken through the boundaries of your fears. You can make all the right moves and still lose; but you can't make no moves and win. Simple ain't easy. The American Dream is not what it seems. We don't fear the loss of things; we fear the loss of what things might mean to us in some distant, hypothetical future. When all our material possessions fade, only love remains. Our memories are our best possessions. Don't decorate the walls of your prison cell; you might not want to leave. People often avoid the truth for fear of destroying the illusions they've built. Minimal is more. The richest man in the graveyard still resides in the graveyard. A man's money does not determine a man's worth. Possessing a pulse doesn't necessarily mean you're alive. A Rolex will not buy you more time. We feel the most alive when we face our deepest fears. Debt, stress, discontent—the worst things in life cost more than we can afford. As long as love is free, you're richer than you know. A man must fall before he can get back up. Karma is a patient bitch. Sometimes we must get cut to discover why we bleed. You are more than just another brick in the wall, but you are not a unique snowflake. Life is brief, but it contains everything. When everything is lost, then there's everything left to gain. Sometimes everything you ever wanted turns out not to be what you wanted at all. We are all slaves to our own opinions of ourselves. Fear hides the key to the door that leads to happiness. There is a direct relationship between your ability to handle uncertainty and your happiness. It's easy to stay where you feel safe, but it's hard to grow from that place. Learn from the past, don't live in it. Nothing is lost. Don't use the past to batter the people you love. Don't build your world around the fault lines. Be tender with the truth. People are often blinded from the truth by the facade of their desires. You are what you consume. What you think affects how you feel; your brain and your body aren't standing in opposite corners of the room. You have to go through what you can't get around. If you settle, you are not going to be happy. *Sacrifice* is not a good thing; neither is *compromise*. If you are careless with something for long enough, it breaks. There's no way to move forward without first changing yourself. Don't look for a sign—look for the right direction. Believe half of what you see, none of what you hear, all of what you feel inside. You have to follow your heart, even when you might lose, for you can lose only once; if you don't follow your heart, you may lose 100 times. It's OK to be confused; being confused means you are open to learning something new. Difficult times add clarity to life—you must step away from the trees to notice the beauty of the forest. Whatever you are looking for, it isn't on your computer screen. The easy route is often not the right route. Sometimes you have to find the good in goodbye. If you wait to live, you begin to die. Not deciding is a bad decision. We spend much of our days attempting to find meaning in meaningless things. Your character is shaped by struggle. Let not your troubles be too troubling. Without worry, you have nothing to worry about. Repetition is the mother of habit. Repetition is the mother of habit. Repetition is the mother of habit. Repetition is the mother of habit. Repetition is the mother of habit. Discomfort is mostly mental. Real rebels risk disapproval. Jealousy is life's weakest emotion. Tomorrow's pleasure drastically outweighs the ephemeral pain of today. We can hold on to only that which we can experience. The more you allow other people to make decisions for you, the less happy you'll be. Funny thing about Time: she'll rob you blind if you let her. We are all experts of the past, novices of the future. Don't wait for someone to tell you that these could have been the best days of your life. Get a fucking life, *your* life, not someone else's template of what they think your life should be.

THIS MAY HAVE BEEN A MISTAKE

Chase Night
Age 30

I was asked to write an essay on the topic "Advice to My Eighteen-Year-Old Self." I immediately agreed. Not because I knew exactly what I wanted to say to my eighteen-year-old self, but because I am a writer addicted to seeing my words in print.

This may have been a mistake.

I have been trying to write this essay for two months. My hard drive is littered with crumpled balls of data that didn't quite reach the recycling bin. Now—with a deadline looming— I have no choice but to confess that I have absolutely no idea how to talk to my eighteen-year-old self.

He doesn't get my Harry Potter references. He listens to the Backstreet Boys without irony. He has no idea that the cast of Dawson's Creek can't act. He can't imagine wanting to live anywhere but NYC. He honestly believes he will win an Oscar for Best Director one day. He is certain he will never try alcohol. He is even more certain that he will never smoke weed. He assumes he is a Republican. He fantasizes about joining the Air Force. He is seriously worried that September 11th was the beginning of the Biblical Apocalypse.

About the only thing we do have in common is that we have never watched Doctor Who. Him because it hasn't been rebooted yet. Me because I've had commitment issues with television series after what happened on Buffy. This strikes me as a little bit ironic since—from what I've gathered online—the Doctor's relationship to his previous incarnation is much like my relationship with mine.

I have his memories—both happy and oh-shit-that's-fucked-up. I have his scars. His residual shame. His question marks. I have fragments of his personality.

But that's where it ends. We don't dress alike or wear our hair alike or walk alike or talk alike. We barely even look alike. We certainly don't think alike.

One day he will become me, but it is only in the most technical of senses that I am still him. I have my own memories—both happy and oh-shit-that's-fucked-up. I have my own scars. My own shame. My own question marks. My own personality that grew around the remnants of his.

These things are mine. They can never be his. I am an entirely different person.

To go back in time and offer him even the smallest piece of advice would be unfair to him. Should I tell him the economy is going to crash when he is twenty-five so it would be smarter to finish college now than to follow his girl to New York? Should I tell him it's better to avoid using credit cards than to swim with sea lions or buy a beautiful Appaloosa horse or drive from Texas to Maine with his girlfriend, two dogs, and three cats? Should I tell him to never quit his job and start a blog because it will essentially bankrupt him?

I don't feel right telling him any of that. He might only be eighteen, but he's got enough on his plate already without me scraping my shit on top of it.

I can't ask him to make up for my mistakes. I can only let him make them. That's his job. He's a dumb-ass kid.

But if I have to offer him some sort of advice—because that is the title of this book after all—I will say this: Fuck up. Fuck up hard. And when you think you can't possibly fuck up any more, fuck up again. Fuck up in the most spectacular ways you can imagine. I will be here to fix it. That's my job. I'm a grown-ass man.

QUARTET

Meg Wolfe
Age 58

I. 28. It's ten years since you turned 18, and you're holding a big baby boy while looking down at a pastel drawing that has just been ruined by dog slobber. The day itself feels ruined. Life feels ruined, or at least going *nothing* like you'd envisioned. All those endless days of inspiration and flow that you experienced in college seem to have trickled to a stop, and instead there are only rare patches of creativity that resemble what you once thought you were capable of doing.

You are no longer nurtured in the closed world of the undergraduate, where you blossomed and found both vision and voice—and suspect, now, that it was all a lie.

You want to go back in time and tell yourself: *They will flatter you in school because they want your tuition money or they want to sleep with you. Open your eyes!*

The output is now so hard to achieve, the encouragement so sparse. You circulate within a different, harsher, more competitive group now. They chip away at your sense of self until you feel *nothing* you do is good enough, and you find yourself frantically racing to be good at it all: a perfect roast beef has the same value as a well-wrought poem.

You want to go back in time and tell yourself: *Have the courage to believe in yourself, in your vision. Even if it isn't bringing in any money. Don't be pushed around by your spouse, your parents, your friends. Insist on having the space and time you need to do your work. Then do it.*

You tell yourself that now, in fact, but it feels like it is too late.

In anger and bitterness, you begin to write dark realizations, and they are so dark that you suddenly stop, because they only get you into more trouble with your people. You have a baby, you feel vulnerable. So you stick to the art, which is so much less literal. The third draft of a novel goes into a box in the basement with the others.

II. 38. The pile set out for pickers and collection stretches across the entire front of the lot, and in places is higher than your head, a one-house landfill of clothes, furniture, housewares, and detritus. Flood, divorce, desperation—you are driven to move away and forced to deal with the debris, both physical and emotional. Notebooks, manuscripts, half a lifetime of words are reduced to stained, moldy pulp, destined for a landfill and not a publisher. And yet you aren't sad, you are ecstatic with catharsis, unloading those old stories, virgin efforts, ready to move on and get real. You see your son, the tired and sweaty little kid with whom you have embarked on a mission of survival and experience. He is bringing out another box. The box has your paints. You add them to the pile with the canvas rolls of paintings taken off their stretchers.

On the twentieth anniversary of turning 18, you wish you could go back in time and tell yourself: *choose your people wisely*. You still don't know if you'll succeed, but you haven't got the luxury of doing things any other way: it's sink or swim. You manage a dog paddle. You write, in secret, just for yourself. You even manage to rewrite one of the short stories, and think it's better than it was before the flood, but that might be because there's no one around to read it. You're afraid that you don't know how to choose friends wisely, so you avoid choosing any at all.

You rethink your skill sets and find work, each job providing a little more information, a few more ideas, quite a few more troubles and problems to solve, and countless more decisions to make, and you learn, a bit late, how the real world ticks, the world outside the keyboards, notebooks and easels. It's the world that begins to form stories in your head, and you realize that, up to now, you really hadn't much to write about at all.

III. 48. You've made some good choices, and some terrible ones. With each crisis, you learned that this, too, shall pass. When the nest was empty, you filled the empty time with reading, writing, and painting—you couldn't not. A wonderful thing called the Internet let you make friends all over the world on your own terms; one of them is now sharing your studio, your home, your life.

But the economy falters, then fails. Your health challenges you in mysterious ways. You find yourself part of a crowded chute of middle-aged people sliding down into difficulties. You write furiously in journals to assuage the stress, which comes and comes and comes with one thing after another. You haven't the stamina to do what you believe needs to be done, and your soul feels so tired. You wish you could tell yourself, *Don't take everything so seriously—have fun, be light of heart, take chances.*

You find it hard to do those things now, because you never really learned how when it would have been natural, like when you were 18. You try to tell your 22-year old son the same thing, but he's not hearing it either.

The pile outside the house grows, eerily similar to the one not so many years ago. You are moving again. *Don't buy so much stuff, you would tell yourself if you could do it over again. Save every penny you can, or at least spend it on something more fun than all this ultimately useless stuff.*

IV. 58. On the fortieth anniversary of turning 18, you bury your father. There were other demanding voices besides his, and those have gone quiet, as well. The sense of time running out is creeping up; you slow it down by immersing yourself in work that fascinates you, working deeply and slowly and seeing method, pattern, and solutions evolve in the process. This was not your youthful way of writing. Strength is replacing passion, new words are quickly surpassing the old.

The Internet is a writer's dream, making publishing possible with a speed and freedom that was unthinkable even a mere ten years ago. You wish you could have told yourself when you first started out, *Don't give up—keep everything you write, you will know how to make it better someday and you will be able to publish it.*

But then you think about it a little more, and realize that *it doesn't matter* that you weren't able to keep the old work, from when neither your heart nor your mind were entirely your own. And *it doesn't matter* if you saved every penny, if you had more fun when you were young, if you chose your people wisely, if you didn't believe everything everybody told you or if you took your work more seriously, because *it all had to happen the way it did.*

The way it happened formed what you have to say now and the way you say it.

One day, you might be holding your son's baby, watching the saga continue, the meaning of things evolving as the world changes. And maybe you'll have a fiftieth anniversary of turning 18, requiring new things to be written.

Happy Birthday to You, and Many More.
And don't forget to have some fun.

Ditto!

Hey Buddy!
I would tell myself
at 18 — Find your tribe!
The people who Root for you
+ stand by you — they are your
tribe! Be good to them too. Treat
everyone with kindness + will come
back to you ten-fold.
Oh — and do some
stupid crazy things!
you'll love having
the stories
later — Kim

13

REMEMBER NUMBER TWO

Hetterte!

Markus Almond
Age 33

It was 4 o'clock in the morning when my friend Josh called me. "Markus," he said. "You've got to go. There isn't much time. Do you have the list?"

"The list!" I shot up out of bed and turned on the lights. "Yes, I have it right here. Where is he?"

Josh gave me an address for a hospital. I threw on some clothes and ran to my rental car. As I sped down side streets and took turns without slowing, I couldn't help but wonder if it was going to work. Josh and his team had put together a project that involved practical research in quantum physics and wormhole mechanics. But every time he tried to explain it to me, I told him that it was far beyond my cognitive abilities. I only hoped that the person I was supposedly meeting would actually be there.

I screeched into the empty parking lot and turned off the engine. The hospital loomed over me as I ran for the entrance. Bright light shined out of every window. When I stepped inside, there was nothing but a large white sign that said, "Markus – 14th floor."

I thought of nothing while I rode the elevator. I held the list tightly in my shaking hand. When the momentum slowed and the elevator doors opened, my heart dropped. I stepped out into a brightly lit waiting room. There were rows and rows of empty chairs. And in the corner of the room with his back turned to me, was the 18-year-old version of myself. It was me from the past. Or maybe I was him from the future. Whichever was true, Josh's experiment had worked.

I couldn't believe I was looking at a teenage version of myself. I forced my legs to move toward him. I felt sick to my stomach. Every cell in my body wanted to stop and run the other way. It didn't seem natural to go back in time and have a conversation with myself. Everything about this plan seemed to defy physics. But Josh had trained me. We had practiced it a thousand times. This will be helpful, I told myself. Don't be afraid of this little punk.

I walked to the corner of the room and sat down next to him. My hands and my crumpled piece of paper were shaking so badly I had to rest them on my knees.

"Hello," he said.

"Hi," I said. I couldn't believe it was happening. He spoke to me. He sounded so young.

"Do you know the old man?" he asked.

"What old man?"

"The old man in there." He pointed to a closed door on the other side of the room.

"I'm not sure," I said.

"I'm Markus," he said.

"Markus," I said shaking his hand.

"You look familiar, man. Have we met before?"

"Not exactly," I said.

"Do you want a cigarette?"

"I don't think you're allowed to smoke in here," I said.

"It don't matter. Ain't nobody here but us." Even the reception desk in the front of the room was empty.

I took the cigarette from him and he lit it for me. The smoke filled my lungs like a termite infestation. I coughed instantly.

"First time?" he asked.

"It's been a while," I said.

"I hate these hospitals, bro. It smells like death in here. Man, you look really familiar," he said.

It was time. I had practiced this. I had my list all prepared. I was ready. I was ready. I needed to do this.

"Can I be honest with you?" I said, unintentionally crushing my list into a tiny, sweaty ball. "I'm actually, um… We're actually the same person."

My teenage-self looked unimpressed and blew smoke across the waiting room.

"I'm you from the future," I said.

He eyed me up and down without saying a word. I looked at him and remembered throwing out the T-shirt he was wearing. "Are you kidding me?" he said. He threw his cigarette on the linoleum tiles. "Shit! Look at you man! We look exactly the same! Oh my God! You're from the future? We could be brothers!" He started laughing and almost dancing. He hugged me and patted me on the back. It felt so strange—like talking to a son or a mirror that could talk back, or maybe completely losing my mind.

I opened up my crumpled piece of notebook paper and put out my half-smoked cigarette on the floor. "I have some things I need to talk to you about."

"How old are you? You look old. Do you have a time machine? Are there hover boards in the future?"

"We don't have time for that stuff," I said. "I have a list of things I need to tell you."

"A list? What kind of list?"

"It's basically some advice and some things I'd like to share."

"Advice? Advice about what? Actually, yeah, go ahead. Let's hear the list."

"Okay," I said. "Number One: Be thankful for everything you have in your life."

"What is this shit?" he said. "Let me see this." He snatched the paper out of my hand.

"Number Forty-seven: wear a condom," he read aloud.

"Give it back," I said. "Give it to me!" I grabbed it from him. My nervousness was instantly replaced by anger. I uncrumpled the list and took a deep breath. "Number Two," I said. "Invest in Apple stock."

"What the hell is Apple stock?" he said.

"It's a computer company," I said. "That's really important. Learn everything you can about the stock market. Take every penny you own and buy Apple stock."

He rolled his eyes at me and lit another cigarette.

"Number Three: When a woman tells you she loves you, the wisest thing you can do is take her word for it." He puffed on his cigarette and gazed across the room. "Number Four:

Don't worry about college right now. Go out and travel. Meet people. Fall in love. Don't take your job too seriously."

"This is bullshit," he said. "Are you telling me these things because you never did them?"

"Not all of them," I said. "Well, Number Two, that one is really important. That one and Number Thirty-Seven."

"What's number thirty-seven?"

"Don't buy a house before 2008. You're in a real estate bubble."

"I don't care about any of this stuff."

"This is important. You need to pay attention. Number Five: Don't ever sell yourself short or tell yourself you can't do something. Six: Your most valuable assets are people – not things." I skimmed ahead in my list. I was proud of my list. I had over a hundred things on there. I had everything from how to raise my credit score to how to conduct myself in a job interview. "Number Seven: Don't be arrogant." My teenage self looked terminally bored. "Are you getting all of this?" I yelled at him. "Don't forget Number Two."

"Seriously, bro. You're bumming me out. Look at you with your little list. You think a bunch of rules can help somebody live a better life? You think that list you came up with is gonna make me happier?"

"Yeah, isn't that the point?"

"No," he said. "It's not the point."

"Listen man…"

"No, you listen!" he screamed. "You don't know me!"

"Know you? I am you!"

"You're not me," he said. "Watch this." He ran over to the empty receptionist desk and jumped over it. He bent down and turned on the PA system. "Paging Mr. Asshole. Mr. Asshole

19

from the future. It's time to get your head out of your ass!"

"Knock it off!" I yelled back. He turned on the radio and Iggy Pop's "Lust For Life" was playing at full volume through the PA.

"I got lust for life!" my teenage self screamed. He grabbed a little desktop microphone and shouted into it. "I'm worth a million in prizes!" He pounded his fist in the air and jumped on top of the reception desk.

"Stop it!" I yelled. "There isn't time for this! You've got to let me say what I came here to say!"

"I got lust for life!" he sang back at me, now dancing on top of the desk and swinging his hips like a skinny Elvis.

"Jesus Christ, man!" I threw the list on the floor and ran after him. I lunged toward his legs and tackled him to the ground. "Listen to me you little shit!" I hit him in the stomach and then in the head.

"Ow! That hurt, Captain Asshole! Stop it!"

I pushed him away and tried to catch my breath. He was lying on the floor holding his stomach and rolling from side to side. I pulled the plug from the radio.

"What the hell is wrong with you?!" he yelled.

"Sit down and listen to me!" I picked up a chair and slammed it down in front of him. "Sit!" I screamed. He picked himself up off the ground and collapsed in the hospital chair. I grabbed my list off of the floor. "Take this!" I threw my crumbled piece of advice at him. "Memorize it!" He took out a fresh cigarette.

I couldn't even look at him. "Not everything is a joke," I said, pacing away from him. "There are things you've got to learn if you're going to be successful and happy. You've got to realize that the world just doesn't revolve around you." When I turned back around I saw my list, burning in a bright orange flame as my 18-year-old self held it into the air in a triumphant 'fuck you' to anything responsible. Smoke and flames shot up into the air.

I ran at him.

He threw the burning list on the ground and stepped aside. I dove towards the list. I covered it with my torso and rolled back and forth to suffocate the flames. When I got up, there was nothing left but ash and three lines: Number 152: Try to see other people's points of view. Number 153: Don't ask what people can do for you. Ask what you can do for them. Number 154: Family is important. And then nothing but black ash curled and crumbling in my hand.

"You have no idea what you just did," I said.

"Don't care," he said sitting down again.

"Give me a cigarette," I said. He threw one at me and I pulled up a chair and sat next to him. "What'd you do that for?"

"Because life ain't about no goddamn list."

"So you don't care what I have to say?"

"Hell no. I make my own way in this life."

I shook my head and lit my cigarette.

"Let me ask you something," the teenage punk said. "Are you happy right now?"

"I was before I met you tonight."

"So what's it matter? If I go about my business and make the same mistakes you did, won't I learn from those mistakes?"

"Yeah, but things would be a whole lot easier if you just took my word for it."

"I don't think it works like that," he said. "I could listen to all the advice in the world but unless I learn for myself, it's not gonna help me."

"Number Two," I said. "Buy Apple stock. That will help you."

"I want my own regrets and I want my own life. I don't want your stupid list. You can't just come here and take all the fun out of my life. You can't just show up with all your dumb-ass regrets and expect me to fix them for you." I exhaled smoke and listened to the punk kid speak. "We make our own path," he said. "That's our gift. That's the point. Advice don't mean nothin'."

"Maybe," I said. "But these are things that I've learned. These are things that I know to be absolutely true. And what better person to listen to than a future version of yourself?"

"Because you're getting old," he said. "I could see it when you walked in here. You've lost your edge."

"You know, everybody thinks they can live forever when they're young."

"And when you're old you get scared of losing what you've got," he said.

"That list would have helped you."

"But I got nothing to lose," he said. "And if you take that away from me, I might as well go get a job as an accountant and invest in a cemetery lot right now."

We both heard the door on the far side of the room unlock. It creaked open. We sat and watched as an old man stumbled out into the waiting room. He was skinny, frail and had a gray beard down to his chest. He took tiny steps with bare feet and wore nothing but a hospital gown.

"Young Marks," he said. When I heard his voice, I realized that he wasn't just any old man. He was me from the future. I couldn't believe what I was seeing. There were three versions of me in the same room. "Don't be disappointed," the old man said. "But my body is just too worn out. I'm not going to make it."

"No!" my teenage self cried out.

"Yep, emphysema," the old man said. "You guys should cut back on the cigarettes."

"Oh shit," my teenage self and I said at the same time.

"It's okay," the old man said. "I've lived a long and fulfilling life thanks to the both of you. You both are on the right track. I think, young Markus, you can be too reckless sometimes. Try not to approach things like you're the strongest man in the world. And you sir," he said looking in my direction, "remember to be thankful. Don't let yourself get lost in the details of life."

"But what if we make the wrong choices?" I asked.

"Commit yourself fully to your decisions and happiness will follow." The old man held a permanent smile on his lips. Even though he was now dying, his smile seemed to be part of him. And hidden in his wrinkled face, were bright blue eyes that still shined with life.

I nodded.

"I have to go now, young Marks." He started walking back towards the hospital room. "Do not fear death." He smiled even bigger. "It's a complete liberation from all hindrances."

And just like that, he walked back and closed the door behind him. The lights in the waiting room started to flicker. From behind the door we heard the old man shout, "Lust for life!" and then there was nothing but silence. He was gone.

"That was messed up," my teen self said.

"Yeah."

"He smelled like an old person."

"Yeah."

"Do you think he believes in Jesus? I think all old people try to believe in Jesus when they get old. It makes things less scary when death comes a knockin'."

My cellphone buzzed in my pocket with a message from Josh that read, "Time's up. Conditions unstable. Leave immediately."

"I've got to go," I said. "Are you going to be okay?"

"Don't worry about me," he said. "I'll be fine."

I nodded.

"I'll check out that Apple stock."

"Actually," I said. "Don't worry about that shit. You've got your whole life ahead of you."

I NEED TO TAKE THIS THING THAT I LOVE AND GET RID OF IT IMMEDIATELY

Josh Wagner
Age 37

Can you feel it? You've crossed the peak. For a long time you've been climbing up, pushing against gravity. Now it's all downhill. You finally got the thing you've always wanted and it turns out having it is nothing like wanting it. Toward the end there you started to develop a real taste for the wanting. That window of time where you knew you were closing in, where you could almost touch it. Right before you pounced. And hey, look at you—you got it. But in your hands it doesn't feel the same as it "almost" did. Feels funny, tastes weird. It's heavy. Looks different, too. Not quite the same shape you saw from a distance. What the hell are you doing? You can't carry this. It fills your arms, obstructs your vision, affords no space for wanting more.

But you want to want more.

You thought you loved this thing but really you loved the arrows that were burning around you as you circled the wagons. And now your entire focus becomes how do I get rid of what took me so long to achieve? Because it no longer feels like the end all be all of your entire life. Now it feels like guilt and confusion and naturally you have to wonder if you're completely broken as a human because aren't we supposed to want something and then have it and then we're happy? But what you've forgotten is you don't actually have it. We never have anything.

Here's the painful truth you already know. Nothing lasts. Everything ends. The only eternal element in life is change. We call phrases like this cliché and roll our eyes when we hear them because we hate it. We hate that we're going to die. In the morning we're pushed out of the airplane and by sunset we'll be a memory on the sidewalk.

So what to do on the way down?

If something has an expiration date you can let it spoil or you can turn it into fuel. What you have now in your arms, what you've struggled so hard to achieve, is ready fuel. You know you can't keep it so you have two options: you can put it in a landfill or you can set it on fire.

Set it on fire.

You don't have a choice as to whether your best days will end up devoured by time, but you do have a choice about how it's done. You can waste it with passion, or you can waste it with doubts and regrets. Stop fooling yourself into thinking it lasts forever. That's the thought that makes you panic, that ignores and denies your natural restlessness and turns it into careless impatience. Embrace your mortality, but don't just sit there like

26

a nihilist and moan about it. Don't pour the oil back into the well. Strike it against a rock until you see sparks. Build the fire, tend the fire, and when the fire goes out don't sit there sifting through the ashes. There's only one time in your life when you can burn all the way down and walk away stronger. Waste your youth. That's what it's for. Don't hold back. Love until it hurts. The fire will fade. You're going to die.

I've got some more advice for you, too.

Ninety-five percent of your fears, doubts, and insecurities only exist in your head. Those people you're so worried about being judged by aren't even paying attention. Only the people who already love you are keeping tabs on what you do. Everyone else is too busy worrying about what other people think of them. Take risks, no one is watching.

The so-called "real" world is a labyrinth of head-games and monkey tricks. Most of these can be sidestepped with confidence and eye-contact.

All confidence is false confidence.

The gloomier things get the more valuable laughter becomes. This is basic economics. Practice laughter, she's your most powerful ally.

Don't be afraid to fight. But first make sure you know how. Don't be afraid to love. But first make sure you don't think you know how.

If you're going somewhere you've been before, take a different route to get there. Ruts are fearsome double-headed dragons devouring time and vitality. And you've got devouring of your own to deal with. Get to it. Stop putting all that work into agonizing over the imminent loss of everything you love. Simply love. While it's still right there in front of you. Time not spent burning is draining, every bit of it trickling away at one second per second. Do you want a trail of fire through the sky or do you want a landfill piled up over your bones?

And when you do fall in love—and you will, again and again and again—don't stop falling just because you hit the ground.

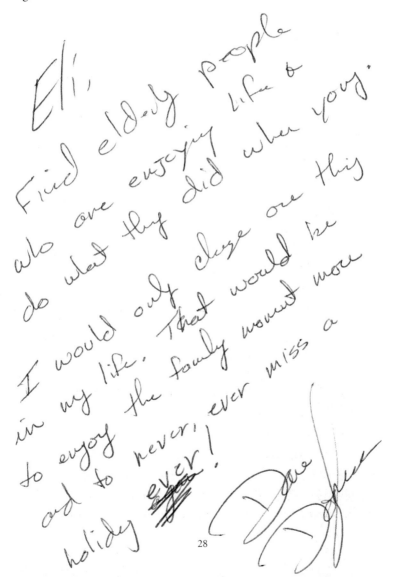

Eli,

Find elderly people who are enjoying life & do what they did when young.

I would only chage one thing in my life. That would be to enjoy the family womant more and to never, ever miss a holiday ever!

Dave

THINGS LIKE

Shawn Mihalik
Age 23

daanaanaanaa nana . . . Batman!

I want to talk to you about superheroes. Because, you see, I know you, and I know you like superheroes. I know you read comic books. I know you travel to the big comic book shows in Akron and Cleveland with your uncle a few times a year.

I know you like Spider-Man, and that's okay because everybody likes Spider-Man, and even way into the future you'll still like Spider-Man, even if they do kill Peter Parker in the most convoluted and literarily annoying way and the series gets stale from that point forward because who wants to see Doc Ock be Spider-Man. I know you don't like spoilers, so . . . sorry for that. And but that's actually the point, the Doc Ock thing, I mean—you like Spider-Man, but the real draw of that particular hero's story is Peter Parker, the geek, the nerd, the secret human that makes all the sacrifices to keep the city safe.

Parker starts out as this normal guy not unlike you, except you don't wear glasses anymore like you did in middle school. And then one day, one normal day, Parker gets bitten by a radioactive or genetically-altered or drug-enhanced spider (depending on the version of the story you read or see) and then it's like, woah, cool, superpowers. And you see this and you think, I want superpowers. Things would be great if I had superpowers. And of course that's actually the same thing Peter Parker thinks when he gets the superpowers, that things'll be great. But in reality the superpowers don't make things any better; they just make things harder. Because when you have superpowers thrust upon you, you suddenly have to sacrifice the fame and the money and the really cool things that come with having superpowers, and you have to use the superpowers purely in the service of others no matter what, ignoring your own happiness and your own desires and sacrificing whatever in the pursuit of good and godly altruistic notions. You would think then, having read past the first issue, that you would no longer want cool spider powers, but really this is even better, you think, because if you're Spider-Man, you're a superhero but you don't have to worry about taking responsibility for your own happiness because that wouldn't be the right thing to do. With great power comes great responsibility, but no personal responsibility, apparently. You connect with the character.

It's the same thing with Batman and Bruce Wayne. And even with Superman—i.e. an outcast, someone not of this planet, someone who doesn't have to be happy, per se, or try to be happy, because his destiny is far greater than happiness. And they've made movies of all these guys—you've seen them. Some of the movies are really good; which is to say you can relate to all these characters, and so can the rest of the world, because they've all been told the same things about life, have had their experience tarnished before they ever had a chance, which is why—and I don't know how to tell you this—they'll make some of these very same movies again, almost literally the exact same movie. They won't be able to get enough.

So you don't value your own happiness, is my point. Or maybe you value it in a way, but you don't expect it to actually be a thing over which you have any control. This has led you to do completely and totally irrational and crazy things.

Things like not tell what's-her-name that you think she's pretty awesome.

Things like take the 30,000 word manuscript about a girl and a boy and dragons and Volkswagen Beetles that you wrote and put it away as if it'll never be worth anything and store the file for so long that you almost forget about it, almost delete it. You saved that manuscript on a neon-green semi-transparent floppy disk. And I'm going to tell you now that the manuscript does indeed suck, but it has the potential to be so very good.

Things like turn down a threesome. You remember those girls, don't you? We'll call them Stacy and Jane even though those were not their names. Not only were they cool people, both of them with tastes in books and music similar to your tastes, but they were in this experimental phase and wanted to have sex with you. Together, both of them at the same time. Your first sexual experience could have been with two women at the same time, man, if you hadn't turned that down. But oh well. And, hey, you'll be happy to know that they're together now, Jane and Stacey, like officially together and married.

Things like pray, as if you praying would cause somebody

you'd never seen or met or been shown any real tangible evidence of would do things for you while you stood there praying all the time just because you asked nicely and even though you failed to make any effort besides pray, which is to say no effort.

Things like eat Little Debbie Snack Cakes and drink a bottle of Southern Brew Iced Tea every day at lunchtime. (And I'm sort of obligated to let you know that you're going to get briefly rather fat from this. Well, from this and the caesar chicken wraps. And the lack of exercise. See, what'll happen is you'll go to college on the back of a mix of a journalism scholarship, a couple grants, and generous financial aid, and in the university's main sort of physical social hub/study center you'll discover this bagel stand that serves Seattle's Best Coffee and chocolate chip muffins and fried chicken Caesar wraps. Every Tuesday/Thursday before your 8 AM myth lit class— which class, along with its professor, who will be a brilliant man and published poet, will indeed inspire you—you'll get the muffin and coffee, and every Monday/Wednesday/Friday, when all your other classes are scheduled, you'll get the coffee and the fried Caesar wrap at lunch time. And you won't exercise, so you'll get fat. And you'll drop out of college after two semesters on the encouragement of apocalyptic fundamentalists, but you'll still be at least 50 pounds overweight for a while.)

Things like buy a blue Pontiac Sunfire with a pink stripe on each side. Your first car. A car which you drove often but never serviced.

Things like never learn how to change the oil of your own car or how to take your car in for someone else to change the oil.

Things like blame the devil for breaking your car when the

engine coughed and sputtered and died on the interstate and left you stranded on your own on the side of the interstate in the rain until a "friend" came and picked you up and with you blamed the devil for breaking your car. Before you could get back to the car later that day with a tow truck, the money for which you scrounged, someone broke in and tore apart the dash and stole your GPS and Bible, which made you wonder if maybe the devil didn't break your car but God broke your car instead so that someone could steal the Bible and find Him. And that just left you confused, you will admit a few years later.

Things like pray for a new car because the devil or God broke your car because he hated you more than a thief or loved a thief more than you, respectively.

Things like accept it blindly as truth when people tell you that all these things happen to everybody all the time, that life is not a pleasant experience, that these things are part of living as a human being in a world shot to hell, that sacrificing amazing experiences and the pursuit of epic goals is noble, is good, is in your best personal interest.

You will get over all that. I can't tell you how, because that wouldn't be fair, because that would rob you of valuable life experience or something, and it would probably break some sort of arbitrary rule of space-time. You know the kind of rule I mean: the kind that applies to one time-travel situation but for some reason doesn't apply to another, based of course on the needs of the plot. In this case the plot demands I not tell you how, but there are other things you will do years after all that. Things that are great and wonderful.

Things like move to the city—twice, because the first time

will be a learning experience—where you'll drink all sorts of artfully-crafted beer, where you'll see all sorts of concerts like Damien Rice and Doctor Dog (who you'd never heard of but the concert was free and in your favorite park so you went and damn) and Augustana (who will have their power turned off by the venue's officials because the concert will go too late and so everyone will leave but when only about 50 of you are still there the band members will say, "Screw it," and play the rest of the night acoustic in the smallest and most intimate show you've ever seen), and where you'll meet all sorts of people and go swing dancing on Saturday nights and salsa dancing on Sundays.

Things like revisit that 30,000 word manuscript, cut out ten words and rewrite the other twenty, submit it to a publisher with whom you've become friends and will eventually become great friends, and ultimately get it published to five-star reviews.

Things like learn to ski and almost break your leg.

Things like read *Infinite Jest* and *A Supposedly Fun Thing I'll Never Do Again* and the rest of David Foster Wallace's unfortunately short body of work.

Things like learn the meaning of art in all its forms.

Things like create art.

Things like learn to play the ukelele. You'll decide that everyone should learn the ukelele. You'll realize that the problems in this world that do exist—problems that aren't nearly as pervasive as you'd been led to believe—would be quote mitigated unquote if everyone played the ukelele. Your favorite songs to play will be "Somewhere Over the Rainbow," "Tonight You Belong to Me," and the theme from Adventure Time.

Things like full sets of pull-ups, pistol squats, and one-arm push-ups. You will work on handstand push-ups, but at this point in my life I can't tell you with certainty if you'll ever do one, although that—to do a handstand push-up—is the goal.

Things like learn to love to climb everything.

Things like give time and cash to charity, which you couldn't do before, because the irony of altruism, you'll learn, is that you seek nothing for yourself and therefore have nothing to give to others.

Things like...

— My husband sure does.
-Kim

Things like still love superheroes. Things like still go to comic book conventions, and you'll realize that the ones you went to when you were young weren't the big ones but only moderately sized. You usually won't buy anything at them because you'll prefer to get comics digitally now, but you'll go there for the people, for the human interaction, for the experience of being around other people who've discovered the same art you've discovered, and also because you've been asked to sign some books there yourself, which is pretty cool and a dream come true and, while it's only for that manuscript that you revisited, someday maybe will be for your own graphic novel.

Things like, while most people continue to love and relate to Spider-Man and poor good ol' Peter Parker and see the third and fourth remake of his story on film, relating more to Iron Man instead, because Iron Man makes awesome things and witty jokes and love and cocktails and, while sure he has to face like really serious stuff from time to time, he, like, kicks, like, legitimate ass.

Things like kick legitimate ass.

Things like turn out far better than you were ever told was possible.

EIGHTEEN YEARS AGO

Robyn Devine
Age 36

At thirty-six, you'd think I've got it all figured out, know where I'm going and how I'm getting there, and be able to feed myself along the way. However, in the years since I was 18 I have learned that I'll never have it figured out, I'm not sure where I'm going or how I'll get there, and we'll probably have to stop for pizza along the way because I didn't pack enough snacks.

Eighteen years ago I was about to graduate high school, and assumed by the time I was thirty-six I would have everything figured out. I knew I was about to embark on a journey that would have me changing the world, helping people, and obviously kicking ass and taking names while living a large and well-known life.

I never expected I'd be married or have a family, own a home, or be totally satisfied to have a practically anonymous existence surrounded by cats, trains and trucks, and the people I love.

If I could talk to that girl about to graduate high school I would say:

Go to the yarn shop with Cara the very first time she asks. While you'll think it strange someone would spend all their time and extra cash on this hobby, knitting will change your life for the better.

Don't beat yourself up for the choices you make. Sometimes those choices will seem counter to how you were raised, what you have always believed, what your family and friends are doing, and what you thought you'd want. That's the way it's supposed to be, so there's no sense in feeling bad about it. You are making the right choices for you.

When you move to Omaha, you will spend a large portion of the first year wondering if you've made the right choice. This will result in what you lovingly refer to as "the breakdown of 2001." Roll with these feelings, as they will shape the woman you will become.

Skinny jeans are amazing. Your friends are right. Don't mock them for wearing them.

Practice kindness with everyone you meet.

Pay attention to the financial advice folks give you. Money will be the one thing that causes you the most stress as you get older, so for the love of God STOP SPENDING SO MUCH OF IT!

Hug your little brothers every chance you get, even when they don't want you to, even when their faces turn red in embarrassment at their older sister who keeps grabbing them into her arms and smelling their hair. Far too soon these little boys will become men and will scatter themselves all over the country, and you'll long for those hugs.

One day you'll wake up and you'll be a mama. I know you think you never want to have children, but trust me when I say one day you will ache for children so badly you don't know if the desire can be contained in your body. And with that ache will come the heartbreak that having children isn't as easy for you as it is for others – don't let that stop you. You are strong enough to handle what will come, and it will be more than worth it. And then you'll get to spend your life picking up stinky socks and tripping over trucks and you'll love every minute of it.

Learn to forgive.

Don't let the drama that having female friends can bring draw you too far away from them. It turns out having girl friends is one of the best gifts, and the women in your life will teach you countless lessons. You will be amazed at the capacity for love and kindness women can show other women, and you will find yourself moved to tears at the compassion and acceptance of the women in your life.

Every time you feel the urge to give something away, do it. One day you'll drive halfway across the country with all your possessions in your car, and it will feel more freeing than anything you've done to that point.

You will come to learn that making hats and giving them away is your calling, your highest purpose on the planet. No matter how strange you think that sounds or how silly others may think it is, sink into this calling. You will learn to meet God in the stitches you make, the stillness of your soul touching divinity as you work with your hands to better the lives of those close to you and complete strangers.

Right now, in your teenage body, you don't think you're

beautiful. You've spent years watching your friends fall in love while the boys you like tell you they aren't interested, and so you spend your time sitting on the sidelines watching everyone else partner up. But before you know it, men will fall over themselves to buy you a drink, tell you how beautiful you are, and want to spend their lives with you. It may take some time for you to trust your beauty, but give yourself the benefit of the doubt.

Also, wear the short skirt. Wear the tube top. Your legs will never be as gorgeous as they are now, and your boobs will eventually need to be held up by more than happy thoughts. I know you think you're showing too much skin, but I promise you'll still be the most conservative gal in the place.

Embrace coffee. One day, making coffee will be your favorite job. You will smell coffee in your hair, on your clothes, and coming out of your pores for years and will love every minute of it.

Trust your soul to lead you on your spiritual path. Over the next decade you'll lead a group of three girls that grows into a group of twenty, host a gathering of 50 kids who willingly get up at 5am on their summer break to sing and pray and start the day together, and feel your heart break as the ministry you love crumbles around you. You'll move to another state to serve the poor and will find your soul irrevocably changed for the better. You will also meet God—not inside a building and not in the books people find sacred, but in the faces of the poor, in the service of others, and in the simple work of turning string into hats using two knitting needles. Your spiritual path will wind and curve and you'll wonder if you've wandered far away from where you were supposed to be, but know that you are walking exactly where you are supposed to.

You will not always be able to dance the way you do now, so dance as much as you can, as often as you can.

In a few months you'll get your first e-mail address, a long and cumbersome university-issued beast that you'll struggle to remember. You'll hate the black screen with the green characters for approximately three months, and then you'll discover the Internet on the library computers. Your life will never be the same. I promise you'll want to stop using the computer for anything other than writing papers, but power through. Your life will be made better and you'll have friends around the globe, all thanks to e-mail and the Internet.

Harry Potter will make you a better knitter and a better person. There are worse things to be obsessed with.

Eat something that makes you nervous at least once a year. You tell everyone you hate shrimp, going so far as to say you're allergic. But at your wedding reception you'll drunkenly try a bite and LOVE IT. This will blow your food mind wide open.

The first night you meet him, you will know you're supposed to spend the rest of your life with him. Don't be afraid to tell him so; he will think you're crazy and won't be able to leave your side. Marriage will be the hardest and best thing you've ever done, and he is the best person to walk that path with.

You will always be innocent and a bit naive. People will try to take advantage of that; pay them no mind. It is a treasure that you trust everyone, believe the best in everyone, and assume those you meet always have the best intentions. People feel the need to live up to that expectation.

Eli-

If I could go back I'd tell myself - Don't worry so much about what others think about your choices - or if you're good enough to do something. TRY DO. Laugh at YOURSELF and keep going - Let worry go - Don't defeat yourself before you begin the race. Be honest, be on time if you give a time or don't say things unless you know you mean it. TRAVEL, hug your family and call your folks often! DREAM BIG.

Erin

HABITS AND COMMUNITY

Ryan Nicodemus
Age 31

I did a lot of crazy things during my teenage years. I lost my virginity in a tent. I did drugs. I snuck out at midnight to buy a Wu-Tang Clan album. I cheated on a final exam. I got married at eighteen.

However, I wouldn't undo any of these experiences; they made me who I am today.

If I could talk to my eighteen-year-old self, I wouldn't tell him which pains, bruises, and relationships to avoid; I wouldn't tell him to invest in Google or eBay.

Avoiding pain and investing in the right stock wouldn't have helped me with longterm happiness or contentment. Giving my eighteen-year-old self advice on how to get rich would have only allowed me to buy more impulsively; it would have only allowed me to foster even more damaging habits in the long run. Plus, avoiding pain at that age would have just made room for other, more painful experiences later down the line.

Instead, if I were talking to my eighteen-year-old self, I'd tell him the same things I'd tell my thirty-one-year-old self.

You don't need to be rich and you don't need to live a perfect life to feel good about yourself. It's different for everyone, and for me at age eighteen, I needed better habits and a better community in my life.

I had spent my high school years experimenting with drugs, hanging out with popular kids, and doing what typical high school kids do. By the time I graduated high school, I had successfully developed an addiction to drugs and alcohol, and had unsuccessfully developed a plan for the start of my adulthood.

At age eighteen, I continued to live off of impulse and feed the bad habits I picked up during high school. I married my high school sweetheart and those bad habits eventually led to our divorce at twenty-two. After my divorce, I continued down the same path, learning things the hard way until I started to make sense of what I was doing to myself.

If I could get in touch with my eighteen-year-old self, I would tell him to let go of the bad habits, to seek good ones instead. I would explain how developing habits around the ephemeral pleasures the world offers leads to discontentment. Instead of establishing habits around television, partying, and doing what's popular, I would tell my eighteen-year-old self to build habits around health, experiences, and individual growth. Life wouldn't have necessarily been perfect if I lived this way from age eighteen, but at least I would have been able to look in the mirror and feel good about the decisions I made. I wouldn't have had addiction, lust, or love for material things to blame for my discontent and failures.

I'd tell my eighteen-year-old self about community. Alongside our habits, the people we associate with define who we are. The more you associate with people who do drugs, the more likely you'll do drugs. The more you associate with people who are passionate about volunteer work, the more likely you'll be inspired to do volunteer work. So forth, and so on.

UNUSED WISDOM

Robert Isaac Brown
Age 20

When I was eighteen, I chose not to use the wisdom I had at that time. I felt in my heart I was on the right path, and I am now two years older. I was in college at my dream institution and living in New York City. I had been focused on getting to New York City since my tenth grade year of high school.

Life was wonderful; I was the happiest I'd ever been, and I thought I had it all figured out. In my eyes, I was striving—moving very fast to make my dreams come true. Impatience was my best friend; I was rushing tasks, neglecting time with family and friends all while trying to fulfill a vision. In addition, while going to a fashion institution, I grew superficial and put the clothes I wore before my character.

Continuing down my impatient path, I told myself I would spend most of my time sharpening my skills as a writer.

However, this did not happen. Since the age of fifteen, I have been a lover of words, and I knew I wanted to be a writer then. At age eighteen, my awareness of how real the possibilities were for me to make an honest career as a writer opened my eyes. I judged my talents and beliefs on the overnight success of others, and this was the unhealthiest thing I could have ever done. I chased the illusion of overnight success, thinking I was running out of time.

When I thought time was against me, I set out to write early in the morning, during class breaks, after class once I got settled at my living space and before my bedtime. Did this happen? No. I was undisciplined and wrote when "inspiration" would strike. Said another way, I hardly ever wrote. Instead, I watched countless reruns of *Boy Meets World* as I waited for Mr. Inspiration to drive me to my laptop to battle the white page and blinking cursor.

There was a time when I felt uncomfortable explaining to people—and even some family—the literary path I wanted to take. I feared they would not appreciate it—most of them being blue collar, hands-on types—and I was correct; they did not understand and laughed at the idea.

Sometimes in life, a second chance is impossible. What I mean by this: I'll never get a chance to be eighteen again, not that I want to be.

I've learned to never place my happiness in the hands of fickle external factors. Hence, my happiness level will only go up and down—being inconsistent and sending me on an emotional rollercoaster. I've learned to be content, and I now understand inner happiness is the only true happiness. I'm still young, with much more living ahead. However, at eighteen, I should have known better. My patience was tested as I zoomed through that age as if my vision would be fulfilled in one solid year of hard work.

That's not how life works.

Two years after eighteen, clothes are less important. I still enjoy looking neat, but focusing more on building my character than my wardrobe has allowed me to put what I do above what I wear. Instead of wasting thoughts on what to wear, I can use my mind in healthier ways, one being thinking of writing ideas.

Instead of watching countless *Boy Meets World* reruns, writing would have served me better. Instead of accompanying my roommates from Brooklyn Heights all the way to the Upper East Side just to window-shop, writing would have served me better. Instead of waking early to surf the Internet before my 8:15 a.m. class, writing would have served me better.

Eighteen was a pivotal year in my life, and though I'm shedding light on my many mistakes, that age paved the way for me to discover and flourish in my true calling.

The best advice I could give to my eighteen-year-old self: Never worry about those who do not understand what you are trying to do with your life, and never go out of your way to explain the path you've chosen to take, especially if those individuals are too impatient to take the time to understand you.

Eli,

My sage advice to
you is pretty simple:
Trust your instincts
but don't be rash,
have fun but stay out
of debt, and ~~neither~~
never forget your friends
and family!

Happy Birthday
Craig

A LETTER FROM ME TO ME

Samuel Engelen
Age 28

Hi there. It's you. I mean, it's me, but I'm you in ten years. Or rather, you're me ten years ago. Because after reading this, you might be a different person in ten years.

How are you? Actually, I have a pretty good idea of how you are, so I'll tell you a bit about how I am.

First off, I'm still alive. That means that if you take the exact same path, you'll be alive in ten years. Of course, "being alive" is probably not your only goal, so feel free to stray from the path. (Also, you don't know which path I'm talking about, so just forget it.)

Second, I'm not exactly where you expect to be in ten years. But to be fair, you probably don't have a clue where that is anyway. I won't spoil it for you, suffice it to say that it's worth it to stick around.

I was gonna take this opportunity to give you some advice, share with you some of the wisdom and knowledge I've accumulated over the last ten years. But then I remembered you —and I—believe in learning from direct personal experience, and if I were you (which I am) I wouldn't listen to a word I'm saying.

Let that be the first thing on the list. Don't believe anything anyone tells you. Some people have wisdom to share, but wisdom is shared through experience, not words. Words are just the fingers pointing to the moon.

Whether you take note of any of these words or not is up to you. All they can possibly accomplish is plant this seed a bit sooner, help you grow a bit faster, so that ten years from now, you'll be a little bit closer to where you really want to be than I am now. But you'll do just fine if you ignore all of it. I know these sound simple—generic even—but complicating things would only confuse you.

The rest of your life will not be like high school. Let that be a reassurance. In fact, in just a few short years, high school will be such a distant past that you won't even remember who was in your classes.

Epic shit does not just happen. You make it happen. And the sooner you start, the better. Do the things that scare you, because that's how you grow. I can say, without a doubt, that the most epic shit that lies ahead comes from doing the things that scare you the most. And if you start doing those things today, you'll experience more epic shit than I ever will.

On that note, the only time to do anything of worth is today. I hate to break it to you, but that's where your teachers were right. The things you postpone are the things you'll give up. Of course, the things your teachers were referring to are the things you probably should give up. It's also pretty much the only thing they were right about.

Whenever possible, travel. Anywhere, by any means, for as long as you can. On your own. It'll bring more value to your life than anything I could ever hope to write in a thousand letters. You know that claustrophobic feeling you sometimes get? Like your life is taking place in some dark tunnel with a small light at the end that never seems to get any closer? Traveling is like climbing out of that tunnel through a manhole you didn't notice before.

Work out. Stretch. Don't worry about looking like a fitness model or being the strongest guy in the gym. Do it for you. Being healthy is not about adding a few years of old age at the end of your life, it's about feeling better right now, and enjoying the years you have before you hit old age. Oh, and fuck gyms. Learn martial arts or get into boxing or something useful.

Write daily. I know you're into film, but film is just a storytelling medium. Without story it is an empty husk, a bunch of disassociated images that amount to nothing. So write, just for practice. Perhaps in ten years you'll write a better letter than I did now.

I'm inclined to tell you to go easy on the booze, but I'm not your parents (none of that creepy time travel incest going on here), and it would probably make you drink more. There's lots of fun to be had with alcohol, and you should probably have a drink after reading this letter. All I'm saying is that some of the time you spend drinking could be better spent reading an extra book, learning how to program or design, improving your language skills or even getting laid (I know you think you're better at meeting girls when you're drunk, but trust me, you're not).

You're gonna hate me for this, but I don't care. Learn how to make money, as soon as possible. Seriously, stop thinking of money as the root of all evil. I know there are a lot of dicks with a lot of money out there, but money gives you the freedom to pursue the things you love. You don't need to make millions and you don't need to be tied to a job. Running your own business is easier than you imagine.

Don't be afraid to make mistakes. Failure doesn't really exist, it's just a word invented by bullies to scare you into the false security of a job. And as you're probably already figuring out, you'll only regret the things you didn't do.

Tell Dad not to buy that apartment or invest in that medical company. Tell him to buy $10,000 to $20,000 worth of Apple shares instead (they'll hit an all-time low ten days after his birthday) and keep them for about ten years. He can thank me —well, you—then.

That's pretty much it. I think I've said too much already. Just forget you ever got this letter.

Oh, one thing: wear sunscreen.

BLACK PEPPER

James Gummer
Age 40

I eat black pepper now. I didn't eat it for years because a psychic told me not to. He said it was responsible for my heartburn. I was impressed he knew that I had heartburn.

My meeting with the psychic was before Facebook existed. Before Myspace. It was before everything we did was posted online for everyone to see.

So the psychic couldn't have known me from the online world and we had never met in person. I was a walk-in customer.

He told me things about my past that he couldn't possibly have known unless he had true psychic abilities. Either that, or he'd followed me around for years like that crazy chick from high school.

I don't know how he read me, but he was good.

He also told me I'd meet a beautiful dark-haired woman who was fair-skinned and thin; he said she'd be my soul mate. She would be very kind and supportive, and we would grow old together.

He predicted that I would meet her in the fall, because in his vision he could see her wearing the type of vest that's worn when there's a chill in the air.

Fall came. She did not.

I wondered if I'd gotten the message wrong. If I hadn't interpreted it correctly. Because, you know, he really didn't say during which fall she'd appear.

Many more falls came and went. Still no dark-haired girlfriend. I was sad. I also felt silly having invested so much in what a psychic said.

And then one day a lovely blonde ballerina, who I'd met during the summer, took me to Paris for New Year's Eve.

Now, it doesn't matter to me what anyone believes about psychics. All I know is that if I'd stayed fixated on the psychic's prediction, I'd have missed an amazing time.

Ambiguity isn't easy to live with. Going through life not knowing how it will unfold from one moment to the next is scary—certainly for me. I often find that I want to cheat the universe. I want to know what's going to happen before it does, hence my visit to the psychic.

I also catch myself wanting to control things.

But I've learned that if I get too attached to one idea, one path, I'll miss things in life. I'll miss opportunities because I'm not open to them. No one can tell me the secrets of life, or how to live, or what will happen. I have to find out for myself.

I wish I'd had these insights at eighteen years old instead of forty.

I also wish I hadn't spent years of my life avoiding black pepper.

I love black pepper. Me too!

And I no longer get heartburn.

18 WOW! to be 18 again:
first I would go back
to school and finish it.
then Jn. College and get
all my degree's done with
after all that go and enjoy
my self. Travel and enjoy
life. follow the road,
great friends, great time.
be a traviling gypsy!
        Much Love
            Me

KICK ASS AND HAVE FUN

Colin Wright
Age 28

It's an interesting time for you. That's something I could probably say to you at any point in your life, but it's especially true now. You're torn between two personalities—feeling like two different people and unsure of which way to go. That's cool. It'll work itself out. It'll all work itself out.

High school was a strange experience, because by the end you were almost popular. Almost attractive and ambitious. Lots of almosts, and I know you wish there was more solid ground to stand on. Don't worry about it. Almosts are good—they can become anything. Embrace almosts.

There are some things I wish I had known when I was your age, and they kind of run the gamut across topical genres, so I'm going to just jump in and convey as much as possible, without giving away any spoilers.

Perspective is something that is vitally important for a well-rounded person. Being able to see the world from another position is key, and that means travel, interaction with those outside your default social group, and generally breaking a lot of habits you were raised with. The road to a rounder self is long, but worthwhile. Break self-imposed barriers when you can find them, and bend any that are applied to your life by outside forces (until you know whether or not they can be safely broken).

Confidence is an issue for many people your age, and it's something that you'll get a grip on eventually, but not for a while. In the meantime, remember that confidence is about knowing who you are and knowing you can overcome anything life throws at you. It doesn't mean proving you're better than anyone else, and it definitely doesn't mean trying to force your ideas on others. Keep your head held high, but don't look down on anyone. And help others do the same. The only race you need to run is against yourself.

Sustainability is key, and I don't mean environmentally (though that's important too). What I mean in this context is that you need to be able to take care of yourself and be able to reach whatever heights you aspire to without anyone else lifting you up. You'll need to create systems that allow you to make money, grow as a person, and still live life, and you'll need to be able to do it as soon as possible, because the benefits of doing so are exponential.

Take time and think about who you are, what you want to be doing, and how you might be able to get there. Life is full of distractions that will keep you in the present at the expense of the future, and authority figures telling you to optimize for the future over the present. You'll need to work out how to live your life—really *live* every moment of it—while still building toward something greater. It's unlikely anyone will help you do this, so prepare to self-educate a whole lot.

Speaking of self-education, there's so much out there to learn—so many things you can become really great at—and an insanely small amount of time in which to hunt it all down and figure it out. You already like to read, which is great, but that's only part of the equation. Lots of knowledge can be found in books, but facts will only get you partway to your goals—the rest will have to be wisdom, gleaned from actual, tangible life. Put all that book-learnin' into practice and go do something amazing.

Health is not something you've always focused on, but at 18, you're starting to get the hang of it. Keep up with that. Health is something you don't truly appreciate until you don't have it, and the absolute best health plan is to keep yourself in the best shape possible, without dedicating your life to athleticism (unless you aspire to be an athlete—which in this case, I know for certain you don't).

Spending all your time fixating on eating the right things and doing the right exercises keeps you from using the very body you're trying to shape. Spending no time on it will leave you feeling depressed and sick and unable to achieve the goals you're aspiring to. Be healthy, but not obsessive. Enjoy life, but don't over-indulge.

In essence, I'm saying you should seek balance. In all things, not just your diet and workout routines. Sex, drugs, drinking—these are all things that can be amazing or horrible, depending on what role they play in your life. It's easy to get down when things don't go according to plan, but it's taking the reins—taking responsibility for your own damn life—that allows you to make manifest whatever hopes and dreams you've got sitting on the horizon.

The results are your own, whether good or bad, and so long as you refuse to quit and stand back up when you encounter a wall where you thought there would be a door, no one can stop you. Maintain that stride and a balanced lifestyle—one that allows you to enjoy all life has to offer without suffering the worst of the consequences for doing so—and you'll be golden.

Relationships are tricky, but not as tricky as you're making them out to be. There's an established way of doing things, but that doesn't mean it's the right way. Don't be afraid to try new things—experiment constantly in all aspects of your life, but especially relationships—and make sure to communicate really, really well. So long as you and the person on the other end of the friendship, coupling, or whatever are getting as much value back as you're putting in, everything will be copacetic.

If a relationship becomes unbalanced, it's time to reassess and either change the nature of said relationship or drop it altogether. In many cases, though, changing the rules a bit—with the buy-in of everyone involved, of course—can solve a whole lot of problems.

Finally—and this is the most important bit of advice I'm going to give you, so pay attention—this is the only life you've got to play with. You don't get a second go around, and things don't start over when you're older and wiser. This. Is. It.

Make the absolute best use of your time that you can. That means moving ever-forward toward your ideal lifestyle, and being happy now, not just later. Because it would be the worst thing in the world to wake up at 80, look back at your life, and realize that you never got started.

Start now. Today. Make plans and act on them. Do

something cool, don't pacify yourself. Be an active participant and shape things, don't just sit back and watch.

Kick ass and have fun.

Yours truly,

You

Eli -

Make sure you enjoy everything you do. Life is crazy as no matter your decisions, life will keep going. So make sure that whatever decisions you make are what you truely want for yourself. Life is crazy so have fun with it! Follow your dreams and passions and you can never go wrong. Happy Birthday Bud! Looking forward to many more with you!

Bobby + Rachel

Eli,

To start make sure to enjoy life. Life is what you make it. Not... What someone else says it should be. At night go to bed and ask yourself could you have done better? If so then wake up and try to do better. If you have done your best, then you have done a great job. Measure yourself to you not to some else you think is better. Because they are comparing to someone else or maybe you.

Be the Best you can be. as that is

Awesome !!!

love you a bunch

Dave

ABOUT THE AUTHORS

JOSHUA FIELDS MILLBURN is the author of eight books and two unpublishable fish-taco recipes, and he thinks of himself as a fairly average guy. Born in Dayton, Ohio, he lives somewhere in Montana. More: www.asymmetrical.co/jfm.

CHASE NIGHT is a writer and story consultant. Yes, Chase Night is his real name. Lucky bastard. His first love is fiction, and he describes his work as being in the Southern Gothic vein. He also writes screenplays and the occasional essay. More info: www.asymmetrical.co/chase.

MEG WOLFE was born and raised in Indiana, where she still resides. She has observed American culture from the white-gloved 1950s through the days of social upheaval, disco, and power suits, good economies and bad, and was politically active through much of it. Along the way, she acquired degrees in English and Art, a Master's in Liberal Studies, and worked as a cook, writer, college instructor, choir accompanist, blueprint girl, slide librarian, graphic artist, housewife, artist, and owned and operated a landscape design firm, an art gallery, and a custom bakery. More: www.minimalistwoman.com.

MARKUS ALMOND grew up writing songs in a punk band and has featured on over 50 TV shows. After touring the U.S. and making records for over a decade, he moved to New York City. His first novel will be released in March 2014. More info: www.brooklyntomars.com.

JOSH WAGNER keeps his coat closet inside a drawer full of nickels. Every time some gentle soul reads his words he pulls a nickel out and mails it to the "Lads of Santa Fe," a non-profit organization specializing in finding new ways to use molten lead in urban environments. Once the nickels have dwindled to the point where the closet door will freely open, Josh climbs inside to wait for the twelfth passer-by to pass by; then he leaps out and with a hearty "Aha!," terrifies the poor fellow (or madam) out of his or her coat. He wears the coat for twenty-four hours, reveling in his cozy treasure. He hangs the coat up in the closet, shovels in a new legion of nickels, and the cycle begins once more. More info: www.joshwagner.org.

SHAWN MIHALIK was born in San Diego, California, in 1990, and currently lives in Youngstown, Ohio, where he studied journalism at Youngstown State University. He is the author of a poetry collection, a novella, and a novel. More: www.asymmetrical.co/shawn.

ROBYN DEVINE makes hats. Literally. Lots of hats. She also writes and has a bunch of kids. More: www.shemakeshats.com.

RYAN NICODEMUS is a mentor, author, and sandwich enthusiast. More: www.asymmetrical.co/ryan.

ROBERT ISAAC BROWN was born in New Orleans and currently lives in New York City. He is working on his first novel. More info: www.craftandthought.com.

SAMUEL ENGELEN blogs, writes books, travels, and simply explores life with his son, Noah. When he feels compelled, he meditates and produces music. He's also a foul-mouthed, perverted, sparingly charming, cynical optimist. And he's totally addicted to motorcycles. More: www.contradictorian.com.

JAMES GUMMER has no idea what's going on and is learning to be okay with that. He writes in Baltimore, Maryland, where he also teaches drumming, qigong, and meditation. More at www.james-writes.com.

COLIN WRIGHT is an author, entrepreneur, and full-time traveler. He was born in 1985 and lives in a new country every four months; the country is voted on by his readers. Find out more at www.asymmetrical.co/colin.

Dear Eli,
   My advice for you
is to not beat yourself up
when things go wrong.
Tomorrow is another day
and being kind to others
and especially yourself
is so very important.
            Love you!
         Auntie Suzie

53674988R00052

Made in the USA
San Bernardino, CA
24 September 2017